W9-BKN-053

Handwriting: Cursive

Published by Brighter Child®
an imprint of Carson-Dellosa Publishing LLC
Greensboro, NC

Brighter Child®
An imprint of Carson-Dellosa Publishing LLC
P.O. Box 35665
Greensboro, NC 27425 USA

ISBN 978-0-7696-7562-6

12-174147784

Practice by tracing the letter. Then write the letter.

a a a a a a

a a a a a a

a a a a

a a

a a a a a

a a a a a a a a

a a a a a a

o o o a a

Handwriting: Cursive

Name _____

Practice by tracing the letter. Then write the letter.

© 2006 Carson-Dellosa

A B C D E F G H I J K L M N O P Q R S T U V W X Y Z

Practice by tracing the letter. Then write the letter.

Handwriting: Cursive

A B C **D** E F G H I J K L M N O P Q R S T U V W X Y Z

Practice by tracing the letter. Then write the letter.

𝒟 𝒟 𝒟 𝒟 𝒟

𝒟 𝒟 𝒟

𝒹

𝒹 𝒹 𝒹 𝒹 𝒹

𝒹

A B C D E F G H I J K L M N O P Q R S T U V W X Y Z

Practice by tracing the letter. Then write the letter.

Handwriting: Cursive

A B C D E F G H I J K L M N O P Q R S T U V W X Y Z

Practice by tracing the letter. Then write the letter.

$\mathcal{F}$ $\mathcal{F}$ $\mathcal{F}$ $\mathcal{F}$ $\mathcal{F}$ $\mathcal{F}$

f f f f f

Handwriting: Cursive

A B C D E F G H I J K L M N O P Q R S T U V W X Y Z

Practice by tracing the letter. Then write the letter.

Handwriting: Cursive

Practice by tracing the letter. Then write the letter.

$\mathcal{H}$ $\mathcal{H}$ $\mathcal{H}$ $\mathcal{H}$ $\mathcal{H}$ $\mathcal{H}$

h h h h h h

Handwriting: Cursive

A B C D E F G H I J K L M N O P Q R S T U V W X Y Z

Practice by tracing the letter. Then write the letter.

Handwriting: Cursive

Name _____

Practice by tracing the letter. Then write the letter.

© 2006 Carson-Dellosa

Name _____

Practice by tracing the letter. Then write the letter.

$\mathcal{K}$ $\mathcal{K}$ $\mathcal{K}$ $\mathcal{K}$ $\mathcal{K}$ $\mathcal{K}$

k k k k k

k k

Handwriting: Cursive

A B C D E F G H I J K L M N O P Q R S T U V W X Y Z

Practice by tracing the letter. Then write the letter.

A B C D E F G H I J K L M N O P Q R S T U V W X Y Z

Practice by tracing the letter. Then write the letter.

m m m m m

m m m m m

Handwriting: Cursive

Name _____

Practice by tracing the letter. Then write the letter.

n n n n n

m m m m m

Handwriting: Cursive © 2006 Carson-Dellosa

Name _____

A B C D E F G H I J K L M N O P Q R S T U V W X Y Z

Practice by tracing the letter. Then write the letter.

𝒪   𝒪   𝒪   𝒪   𝒪

𝑜   𝑜   𝑜   𝑜   𝑜

Handwriting: Cursive

Name _____

Practice by tracing the letter. Then write the letter.

$\mathcal{P}$ $\mathcal{P}$ $\mathcal{P}$ $\mathcal{P}$ $\mathcal{P}$

p p p p p

Name _____

A B C D E F G H I J K L M N O P Q R S T U V W X Y Z

Practice by tracing the letter. Then write the letter.

Q Q Q Q Q

q q q q q

Handwriting: Cursive

A B C D E F G H I J K L M N O P Q **R** S T U V W X Y Z

Practice by tracing the letter. Then write the letter.

$\mathcal{R}$ $\mathcal{R}$ $\mathcal{R}$ $\mathcal{R}$ $\mathcal{R}$

$\mathcal{R}$

$\mathcal{N}$ $\mathcal{N}$ $\mathcal{N}$ $\mathcal{N}$ $\mathcal{N}$

20

A B C D E F G H I J K L M N O P Q R **S** T U V W X Y Z

Practice by tracing the letter. Then write the letter.

S *S* *S* *S* *S*

s *s* *s* *s* *s*

Handwriting: Cursive

A B C D E F G H I J K L M N O P Q R S T U V W X Y Z

Practice by tracing the letter. Then write the letter.

A B C D E F G H I J K L M N O P Q R S T U V W X Y Z

Practice by tracing the letter. Then write the letter.

U U U U U

U

UU UU UU UU UU

23

Handwriting: Cursive

A B C D E F G H I J K L M N O P Q R S T U V W X Y Z

Practice by tracing the letter. Then write the letter.

$\mathcal{V}$ $\mathcal{V}$ $\mathcal{V}$ $\mathcal{V}$ $\mathcal{V}$

$\mathcal{N}$ $\mathcal{N}$ $\mathcal{N}$ $\mathcal{N}$ $\mathcal{N}$

24

Name

A B C D E F G H I J K L M N O P Q R S T U V **W** X Y Z

Practice by tracing the letter. Then write the letter.

𝒲 𝒲 𝒲 𝒲 𝒲

𝓌 𝓌 𝓌 𝓌 𝓌

Handwriting: Cursive

Name _____

Practice by tracing the letter. Then write the letter.

$\mathcal{X}$ $\mathcal{X}$ $\mathcal{X}$ $\mathcal{X}$ $\mathcal{X}$ $\mathcal{X}$

x x x x x x

© 2006 Carson-Dellosa

Name _____

Practice by tracing the letter. Then write the letter.

𝒴 𝒴 𝒴 𝒴 𝒴

𝓎 𝓎 𝓎 𝓎 𝓎

Handwriting: Cursive

A B C D E F G H I J K L M N O P Q R S T U V W X Y Z

Practice by tracing the letter. Then write the letter.

A B C D E F G H I J K L M N O P Q R S T U V W X Y Z

Practice by tracing the words. Then write the words.

an

and

animals

April

Handwriting: Cursive

A **B** **C** **D** **E** **F** **G** **H** **I** **J** **K** **L** **M** **N** **O** **P** **Q** **R** **S** **T** **U** **V** **W** **X** **Y** **Z**

Practice by tracing the words. Then write the words.

big

big

boy

babble

baboon

A B **C** D E F G H I J K L M N O P Q R S T U V W X Y Z

Practice by tracing the words. Then write the words.

can

candy

cool

count

Handwriting: Cursive

A B C **D** E F G H I J K L M N O P Q R S T U V W X Y Z

Practice by tracing the words. Then write the words.

do

dog

dandelions

dandelions

donuts

A B C D **E** F G H I J K L M N O P Q R S T U V W X Y Z

Practice by tracing the words. Then write the words.

each

eat

eels

eighty

Handwriting: Cursive

A B C D E F G H I J K L M N O P Q R S T U V W X Y Z

Practice by tracing the words. Then write the words.

far

fat

fluff

feast

Name _____

Practice by tracing the words. Then write the words.

gag

gift

good

giggle

Handwriting: Cursive

Name _____

Practice by tracing the words. Then write the words.

his

happy

he

hello

Name _____

Practice by tracing the words. Then write the words.

if if

in in

idea

itch

Handwriting: Cursive

A B C D E F G H I J K L M N O P Q R S T U V W X Y Z

Practice by tracing the words. Then write the words.

jam

job

jazz

junk

A B C D E F G H I J K L M N O P Q R S T U V W X Y Z

Practice by tracing the words. Then write the words.

kid

key

Kick

keep

Handwriting: Cursive

| A | B | C | D | E | F | G | H | I | J | K | **L** | M | N | O | P | Q | R | S | T | U | V | W | X | Y | Z |

Practice by tracing the words. Then write the words.

low

land

lamb

little

A B C D E F G H I J K L **M** N O P Q R S T U V W X Y Z

Practice by tracing the words. Then write the words.

mad

milk

monkeys

merry

Handwriting: Cursive

A B C D E F G H I J K L M **N** O P Q R S T U V W X Y Z

Practice by tracing the words. Then write the words.

nap

name

near

night

A B C D E F G H I J K L M N O P Q R S T U V W X Y Z

Practice by tracing the words. Then write the words.

out

often

once

order

Handwriting: Cursive

Name _____

A B C D E F G H I J K L M N O **P** Q R S T U V W X Y Z

Practice by tracing the words. Then write the words.

pan

pet

pick

paper

44

Handwriting: Cursive

© 2006 Carson-Dellosa

Name _____

Practice by tracing the words. Then write the words.

quit

quick

quart

quiet

45

Handwriting: Cursive

A B C D E F G H I J K L M N O P Q **R** S T U V W X Y Z

Practice by tracing the words. Then write the words.

rat

run

rear

road

A B C D E F G H I J K L M N O P Q R S T U V W X Y Z

Practice by tracing the words. Then write the words.

see

sing

stand

stow

Handwriting: Cursive

A B C D E F G H I J K L M N O P Q R S **T** U V W X Y Z

Practice by tracing the words. Then write the words.

the

tip

told

twist

A B C D E F G H I J K L M N O P Q R S T U V W X Y Z

Practice by tracing the words. Then write the words.

use

under

until

unhappy

Handwriting: Cursive

A B C D E F G H I J K L M N O P Q R S T U **V** W X Y Z

Practice by tracing the words. Then write the words.

very

vote

vine

vest

Name _____

A B C D E F G H I J K L M N O P Q R S T U V **W** X Y Z

Practice by tracing the words. Then write the words.

wet

west

wall

winter

Handwriting: Cursive

Name _____

A B C D E F G H I J K L M N O P Q R S T U V W **X** Y Z

Practice by tracing the words. Then write the words.

x-ray

box

extra

xylophone

X-RAY MACHINE

FOX IN BOX

A B C D E F G H I J K L M N O P Q R S T U V W X **Y** Z

Practice by tracing the words. Then write the words.

you

yard

year

yellow

53

Handwriting: Cursive

A B C D E F G H I J K L M N O P Q R S T U V W X Y Z

Practice by tracing the words. Then write the words.

zero

zoom

zone

zipper

Name _____

Write the sentence.

Arctic animals

act amusingly.

Handwriting: Cursive

A B C D E F G H I J K L M N O P Q R S T U V W X Y Z

Write the sentence.

Big baboons

break balloons.

Write the sentence.

Cool crocodiles count coconuts.

Handwriting: Cursive

Name _____

Write the sentence.

Dogs deliver dandelions and donuts.

A B C D **E** F G H I J K L M N O P Q R S T U V W X Y Z

Write the sentence.

Electric eels eat excitedly.

Handwriting: Cursive

Name _____

Write the sentence.

Flamingos fluff fancy feathers.

A B C D E F G H I J K L M N O P Q R S T U V W X Y Z

Write the sentence.

Giggling gophers give gag gifts.

Handwriting: Cursive

A B C D E F G **H** I J K L M N O P Q R S T U V W X Y Z

Write the sentence.

Happy hippos
hang in their
hammocks.

Name _____

Write the sentence.

Insects itch in the infield.

Handwriting: Cursive

A B C D E F G H I **J** K L M N O P Q R S T U V W X Y Z

Write the sentence.

Juggling jaguars jam to jazz.

Name _____

A B C D E F G H I J K L M N O P Q R S T U V W X Y Z

Write the sentence.

Kooky kangaroos kick in karate.

65

© 2006 Carson-Dellosa

Handwriting: Cursive

A B C D E F G H I J K **L** M N O P Q R S T U V W X Y Z

Write the sentence.

Little lambs lick lemon lollipops.

A B C D E F G H I J K L M N O P Q R S T U V W X Y Z

Write the sentence.

Merry monkeys
make marmalade.

Handwriting: Cursive

Name _____

Write the sentence.

Naughty gnats never nap at night.

A B C D E F G H I J K L M N O P Q R S T U V W X Y Z

Write the sentence.

Ostriches often order onion omelettes.

Handwriting: Cursive

A B C D E F G H I J K L M N O P Q R S T U V W X Y Z

Write the sentence.

Pandas paint pictures on paper.

Handwriting: Cursive

© 2006 Carson-Dellosa

A B C D E F G H I J K L M N O P Q R S T U V W X Y Z

Write the sentence.

Quick quails quarrel over a unique quarter.

Handwriting: Cursive

A B C D E F G H I J K L M N O P Q R S T U V W X Y Z

Write the sentence.

Raccoons run races in red cars.

Handwriting: Cursive

Write the sentence.

Standing storks sing with swans.

Handwriting: Cursive

Name _____

Write the sentence.

Two tigers tickle the other's toes.

Handwriting: Cursive

© 2006 Carson-Dellosa

A B C D E F G H I J K L M N O P Q R S T **U** V W X Y Z

Write the sentence.

Unicorns use umbrellas under thunder.

Handwriting: Cursive

A B C D E F G H I J K L M N O P Q R S T U V W X Y Z

Write the sentence.

Vultures vacuum in velvet vests.

Handwriting: Cursive

© 2006 Carson-Dellosa

Name _____

Write the sentence.

Wet walruses

bowl to win.

Handwriting: Cursive

A B C D E F G H I J K L M N O P Q R S T U V W X Y Z

Write the sentence.

Xandra x-rays boxes with foxes.

X-RAY MACHINE

FOX IN BOX

Name _____

Write the sentence.

Yaks yell and yodel loudly.

Handwriting: Cursive

A B C D E F G H I J K L M N O P Q R S T U V W X Y Z

Write the sentence.

Zigzagging zebras

zip and zoom.